THE GUITAR

THE GUITAR

An Illustrated
Step-by-Step
Instructional Guide

Frank Cappelli

ELDORADO INK

Eldorado Ink
PO Box 100097
Pittsburgh, PA 15233
www.eldoradoink.com

First printing

1 3 5 7 9 8 6 4 2

Library of Congress Cataloging-in-Publication Data

   Cappelli, Frank.
     The Guitar. An Illustrated Step-by-Step Guide / Frank Cappelli.
        p. cm. — (Learn to play)
     Includes bibliographical references and index.
     ISBN-13: 978-1-932904-14-7
     ISBN-10: 1-932904-14-X
     1. Guitar—Methods. I. Title.
     MT582.C17 2007
     787.87′193—dc22
                                        2006035578

Acknowledgements

The author would like to thank all of those who provided instruments to be used in the photographs of this book, particularly Dr. Leo "Fingers" McCafferty and Empire Music of Pittsburgh (412-343-5299; www.empiremusiconline.com).

TABLE OF CONTENTS

Introduction   9

Part One: The Guitar Basics

1. Choosing a Guitar   10
2. Do I Need an Amplifier?   12
3. Holding the Guitar   15
4. Hand Techniques   16
5. Strumming   17
6. The Strings   17
7. Tuning the Guitar   18
8. Changing Your Strings   20

Part Two: Making Music

1. Reading a Chord Diagram   22
2. The G and D Chords   23
3. Reading the Music   26
4. Time Signature   27
5. Rhythmic Notes   28
6. Basic Warm-up   31
7. G and D Exercises   32

8. Reading Guitar Pieces in Tablature 34
9. Two New Chords: C and F 39
10. New Chords: E, Em, and E7 50
11. The Family of A 55
12. One More Chord (B7) 64
13. Playing with the Chords You Know 65

Part Three: Beyond Chords
1. Exploring the Rest of the Basics 74
2. The Notes 75
3. Clef Symbols 77
4. Time Signature 77
5. More Chords 78
6. The Sharp and Flat Signs 79
7. String Notation 80
8. The E (First String) and its Notes 80
9. The B String and its Notes 83
10. The G String and its Notes 86
11. The D String and its Notes 88
12. The A String and its Notes 91
13. The E String and its Notes 94

Part Four: More Songs
1. Kumbaya 98
2. My Bonnie 99
3. Cielito Lindo 100
4. Bingo 101
5. On Top of Old Smokey 101
6. At the Gate of Heaven 102
7. This Old Man 102
8. Red River Valley 103

Appendix: Chord Diagrams   104
Guitar Timeline   106
Internet Resources   109
Glossary   110
Index   111
About the Author   112

Clarinet
Flute
Guitar
Piano
Trumpet
Violin

INTRODUCTION

The guitar is one of the most common instruments in the world. Anyone can walk into a music store, pick up a guitar, and strum it. With this book, you can become not just a strummer but a player. Like all guitar players, you will experience both exhilaration and frustration as you learn to understand and master your new instrument.

This book is structured to make your experience learning the guitar as stress free as possible. The instructions, diagrams, and illustrations will help you through everything from the purchase of a guitar, to its tuning, to the actual playing of the instrument.

Before getting started, remember the most important thing to learning: practice. Practicing at least 20 minutes a day is a good goal to set when starting out. It will help you get a feel for your guitar and enable you to learn and remember the basics. As you become more experienced, you will naturally want to pick up your guitar a lot more than just 20 minutes a day.

I have found the guitar to be a fun instrument, and I hope this book will help you find the fun in learning and playing the guitar.

PART ONE: THE GUITAR BASICS

1. Choosing a Guitar

When looking for a guitar, the first thing to ask yourself is what type of guitar you want. Basically, there are two types of guitars to choose from: an acoustic guitar (which has a hollow body with a round sound hole in the middle) or an electric guitar (which has a solid body and no sound hole). If you want an instrument you can easily take with you and play indoors or out, try an acoustic guitar.

Remember that there is a difference between an acoustic and electric guitar. The difference in body style gives each guitar a completely different feel. When trying to decide whether to start with an electric or acoustic guitar, there is no "right" choice. Whatever guitar you think feels good or will encourage you to play should be for you. One way to help you decide may be to think of your favorite music or artist. That way you will be able to learn to play your favorite songs. If your favorite kind of music is rock, then an electric guitar could be for you. Or if you prefer country, bluegrass, or folk music, then an acoustic would do. Most genres of music use both acoustic and electric guitars.

When shopping for a guitar, it is very important to go out and try different ones at a music or guitar store. Compare the way each guitar feels when you press the strings against the fret board. The strings should not be very hard to press down. Also, don't be afraid to talk to the employees at a music store, because they are usually musicians and love to talk about music. Try asking them for their opinions on the different guitars. In most cases they will be happy to help you. If possible, go to more than one store.

Many companies make guitars. I happen to be very fond of Martin, Gibson, Fender, and Guild guitars.

PARTS OF THE GUITAR

The Head

Tuning Pegs

The Nut

Frets

The Body

Sound Hole

Electric Pickups

Bridge

Volume, Tone, and Pickup Controls

1/4" Jack

Whammy Bar

Acoustic Guitar   Electric Guitar

A small amplifier is probably
best for beginners.

2. Do I Need an Amplifier?

If you decide to buy an electric guitar, then you must also pick up an amplifier. An acoustic guitar does not require an amplifier to make its sound, while an electric guitar will hardly make a sound without one.

You will have many options when picking an amplifier. Use the same methods you used in buying your guitar. Be sure to try a number of different types and pick one that best fits your need. Small, low wattage amplifiers have a nice sound for practicing or playing with a friend. But for playing in a band—when the sound must carry over other musicians or over a distance—a large, high wattage amplifier may be needed. Keep in mind, though, that the larger the amplifier is, the more expensive it will be.

HELPFUL TIP:
For the beginning guitar player, a practice amp is usually the best bet. You can probably find one at the local music store for less than $100.

3. Holding the Guitar

It is important to remember that the guitar should always feel comfortable in your hands. Make sure the neck of the guitar points slightly upwards toward the ceiling.

There are three basic playing positions:

Position A: While sitting down with or without a strap, hold the neck slightly toward the ceiling, resting the guitar on your right thigh.

Position B: Rest the guitar on your left thigh if you are sitting with your right foot propped up on a footstool.

Position C: When you are standing, a strap is needed to help keep the neck pointed in the correct direction (upward).

Position A

Position B

Position C

4. Hand techniques

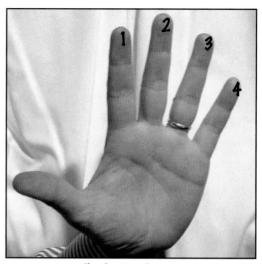

The Guitar Fingers

The Left Hand

The responsibility of the left hand is to press the strings at the correct place on the frets so the guitar will make the desired sound.

The Guitar Fingers of Your Left Hand

Your index finger will be 1, the first finger. Your middle finger will be 2, the second finger. Your ring finger will be 3, the third finger, and your pinky finger will be 4, the fourth finger.

The Thumb

The thumb should be around the back of the neck helping to maintain grip.

Thumb Positioning

Left Hand Positioning

Whether playing a single note or a chord, the fingers on your left hand should be slightly arched so you play with the tips of your fingers. Slightly arching your fingers will help keep them from touching the other strings.

When playing a note, place your finger on the guitar close to the middle of the fret. Do not place your fingers directly on the metal fret. Make sure to always keep your wrist relaxed while playing.

Proper Finger Placement

The Right Hand

The right hand is as important as the left. It provides the rhythm of the song by playing the strings to create the sound.

Most beginning guitar players use a pick. The best way for beginners to hold a pick is to grip it firmly between your thumb and your index finger.

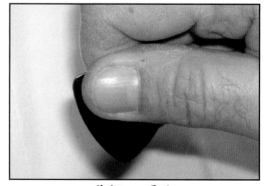

Holding a Pick

5. Strumming

The motion the right hand makes across the strings is called the strum. Gently sweep the pick across the strings in either a downward strum or upward strum. Sometimes the music will have you strum all the strings. But at other times, you will strum just some of the strings. When strumming use only your wrist. Don't move your entire arm.

In musical notation the down strum looks like this:

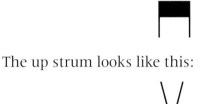

The up strum looks like this:

6. The Strings

Now let's move on to the strings of the guitar. Each string is tuned to a specific note. We'll start with the top string (the thinnest), which is referred to as the first string (and is marked as 1 on the string diagram below). This string is tuned to play the note E.

Standard guitar diagrams such as the one shown here depict the instrument as it would appear in a vertical position, with the strings facing your body. (The horizontal lines represent frets.) Thus the first string is the one furthest to the right.

Moving from right to left—bottom to top if you were holding the guitar in the playing position—the second string is B, the third string is G, the fourth D, the fifth A, and the sixth E. This is the note each string plays when properly tuned: (Sixth) E A D G B E (First)

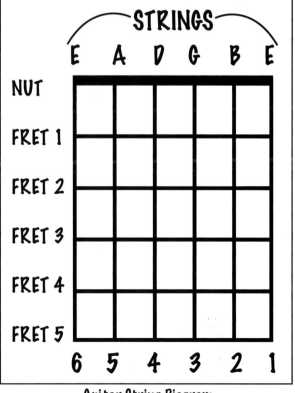

Guitar String Diagram

A pitch pipe can be used to tune a guitar.

Electronic tuners are available at most music stores.

7. Tuning the Guitar

Now we're almost ready to start playing. But before that, the last thing we need to do is tune your guitar. This is to ensure you have tuned each string to the right note.

There are several ways to tune a guitar. One is by using a pitch pipe, which gives a pitch (tone) to match each string. You play the note on the pitch pipe, then turn the peg for that string until the string's tone matches the pitch pipe. Another way is to use an electronic tuning device, which you can buy at most music stores. These devices use either a display screen or a system of lights to indicate whether the pitch needs to be higher or lower. They range in price from about $20 to $100.

Using one of these devices is a very good way to make sure your guitar is in tune. Eventually, you may learn how to tune your guitar without any help from these devices, using a method called relative tuning. But in order to reach that point, you have to know how the strings are supposed to sound when they are properly tuned.

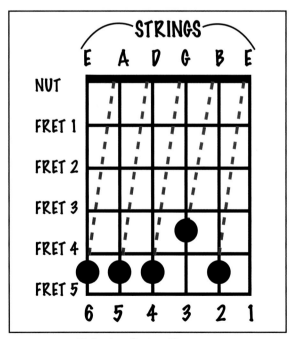

Relative Tuning Diagram

HELPFUL TIP:
It's important to make sure that your guitar is in tune, so that you become familiar with the proper sounds of different chords and notes. If you ever want to jam with other musicians, your instrument will have to be in tune so that you can play in harmony.

Relative Tuning

Relative tuning is "tuning by ear." In relative tuning you need a tone from a tuning fork or the piano.

Using the tone from the tuning fork or piano, turn the peg of the low E string (string 6) until the tone in produces matches the tone from the piano or tuning fork. After this string is tuned, you can tune the rest of the strings.

First, place your 1 finger on the fifth fret of the sixth string. Using the tuning pegs on the head of the guitar, tune the open fifth string to the tone of the sixth string. Do the same with the fifth and fourth string. On the third string, place your 1 finger on the fourth fret of the third string to match the tone of the open second string. Finally, place your 1 finger on the fifth fret of the second string and match the tone of the first or high E string.

You will now have the guitar in what is known as standard tuning. There are several other keys in which the guitar can be tuned, but for now we will be working with standard EADGBE tuning.

8. Changing Your Strings

It's a good idea to have an extra set of strings in your guitar case. You never know when you may break a string and need a replacement. With any guitar it is also good to have a pair of wire cutters and a lint-free cloth in your case. (You can purchase a guitar care kit that contains these items, as well as extra strings, at your local music store.)

Just before you put on a new string, take your cloth and wipe down the guitar, especially where the old string was strung.

If you have an acoustic guitar, take the peg out of the bridge located just below the sound hole (figure 1). Place the little ball end of the string down

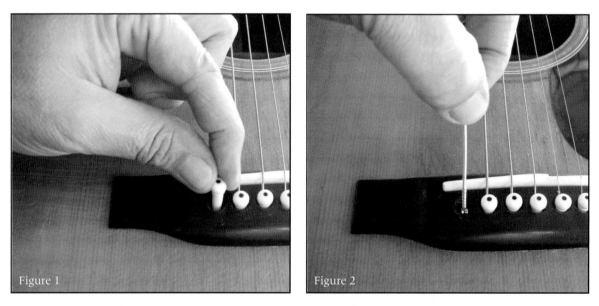

Figure 1

Figure 2

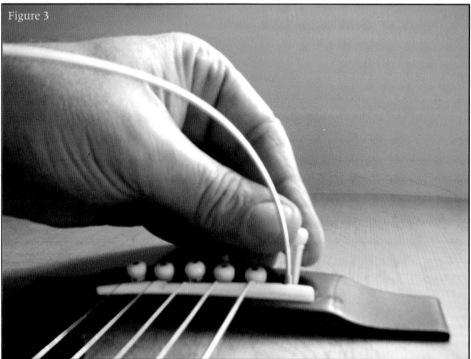

Figure 3

the hole and replace the peg (figure 2). Gently pull up on the string and press down lightly on the peg (figure 3).

Take the other end of the string and feed it through the hole in the tuning peg up on the head of the guitar (figure 4). As you feed the string

Figure 4

through, slowly turn the peg toward you. Keep turning until the string reaches the correct tone. Check every once in a while to see if the peg is coming out of the hole. If it is, gently press the peg back into the hole.

Once this is done you will have a loose string end at the top of your guitar. You can either cut these ends with the wire cutters (figure 5) or curl them into circles. Don't let them hang loose or they may hurt someone.

Figure 5

For an electric guitar, the place where you feed the string through at the bottom often varies with each instrument. If you are not sure about how to change the strings, ask the salesperson to show you. The process of feeding the string through at the top is the same for all guitars.

PART TWO: MAKING MUSIC

1. Reading a Chord Diagram

Now we're ready to start playing! We're going to start off with some basic chords. Before we do that, though, it is important to understand what a chord is.

A typical chord diagram

A chord is three or more notes played at the same time. Chords can be displayed in three different ways: in a chord diagram, which we'll look at now, within the musical staff, or in tablature notation (TAB). In this book, chords will be shown all three ways as you learn them.

A chord diagram shows you where to place your fingers on the guitar to make a chord. Again, in the diagram the guitar is depicted as it would appear facing you, with the vertical lines representing the strings and the horizontal lines representing the frets.

The black dots show where you place your fingers on the fret board. The number at the top of the string tells you what finger of the left hand to use. If you see an "o" at the top, it means play the string "open" (without a finger pressed down on it) when strumming. If you see an "x," it means the string should not be strummed at all when playing that chord.

Notice that the chord diagram appears above the musical staff. Each chord diagram in this book will also show you how the chord will look on the staff, so you get a general idea of what musical notation looks like. Finally, the chords will also be written in tablature, a method of reading music that will be explained in detail on page 34 of this book.

2. The G and D Chords

The G chord:

The 1 finger should be on the second fret of the A, or fifth, string. The 2 finger should be on the third fret of the low E string (the sixth string). The 3 finger should be on the third fret of the first string (the high E string).

HELPFUL TIP for playing G: When playing this chord position your 2 finger high on the third fret. That makes it easier for the other fingers to reach their strings.

The G7 chord

The G7 chord is played by placing your 1 finger on the first fret, first string, your 2 finger on the second fret, fifth string, and your 3 finger reaching all the way across the fret board to the third fret, sixth string.

As you move between the G and G7 chords, your fingers will move more than they normally do. Take your time as your fingers get used to the jump from one chord to the other.

The D chord:

The 1 finger should be on the second fret of the third string. The 2 finger should be on the second fret of the first string. The 3 finger should be on the third fret of the second string.

The x means you do--> not play that string

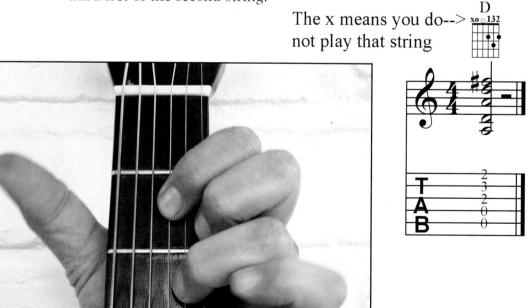

The Dm chord

The Dm chord is played with your 1 finger on the first fret, first string, 2 finger on the second fret, third string, and the 3 finger on the third fret, second string.

The D7 chord

The D7 chord is played with your 2 finger on the second fret, third string, 1 finger on the first fret, second string, and your 3 finger on the second fret, first string.

As you practice, try to memorize each chord. Try this by switching back and forth between the chords you have learned. Practice playing from memory without looking at the diagram, making sure to look at your left hand to see what it needs to do.

3. Reading the Music

Now that you know a few chords, let's try to learn a bit about reading music. It is difficult to get the hang of, but it will give you a better understanding of music and the way it is made.

When learning and writing musical notation, think of it as a language. Think of the staff as the lines on a sheet of paper and the notes as the words.

The Staff

A staff has five lines and four spaces, and the notes placed on it indicate the pitch and rhythm of the music.

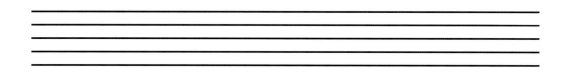

The lines and spaces each represent different notes, as shown below:

To give order to the music, the staff is divided into measures. We use a vertical line called a bar (or bar lines) to make the measures. Here is the staff with bar lines separating the measure.

The double bar line at the end of the staff means that you're at the end of a section or strain of music. When there are two dots before the double lines, it means go back and play from the beginning.

The six strings of the guitar

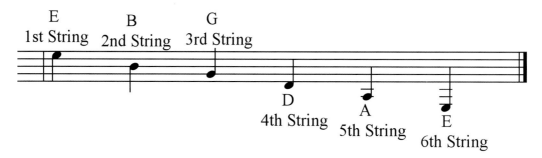

4. Time Signature

Another thing found on the staff is the time signature, displayed here:

2/4 Time   4/4 Time   3/4 Time   6/8 Time
          (also known as common time)

This signature tells us how many beats are in a measure and what note gets one beat.

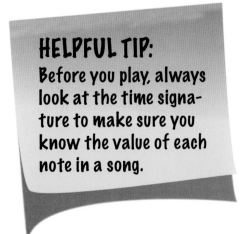

The top number is the number of beats per measure. The 4 here means four beats per measure.

The bottom number indicates the type of note that gets one beat (quarter note, half note, etc.) The 4 here means the quarter note gets one beat.

If the top number was a 6, it would mean there would be 6 beats per measure, and if the bottom number was an 8, it would mean the eighth note gets one beat. Musicians call this 6/8 time.

You will sometimes see a C in the place of a time signature. That simply stands for 4/4, or common time. Most of the music you will see is either in 4/4 or 3/4 time.

HELPFUL TIP:
Before you play, always look at the time signature to make sure you know the value of each note in a song.

5. Rhythmic Notes

Before we start playing more chords, let's start to practice rhythm. Here are the notes you will see when playing chords:

When you see a stem with a slash, this is a rhythmic quarter note. It gets one strum per beat. A rhythmic half note is a stem with a hollow diamond or a stem with a hollow oval. It always gets two beats within a measure. A rhythmic whole note is a hollow oval (or diamond) with no stem. It receives four beats within the measure.

You will only see these symbols when playing chords. We will look at musical notation more in depth later. For now, try strumming some of the chords we've covered, following the rhythmic notation. Remember, when you see the two vertical dots before the double bar on the staff it means you go back to the beginning and play it again.

Repeat Sign

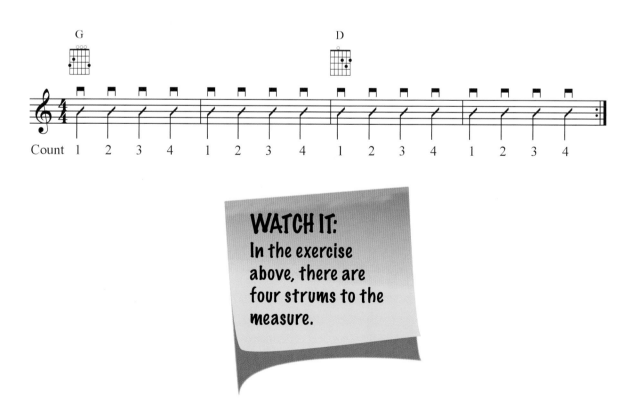

WATCH IT:
In the exercise above, there are four strums to the measure.

In 3/4 time, there are now three beats to a measure, but the quarter note still gets one beat.

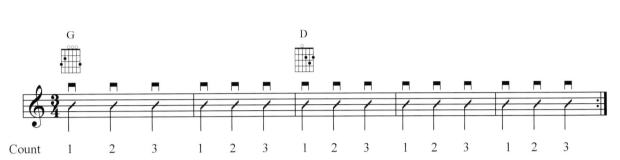

Following are two exercises using half notes. In 4/4 time the half note gets two beats, so there are two half notes in each measure. The half notes are played on the first and third beats.

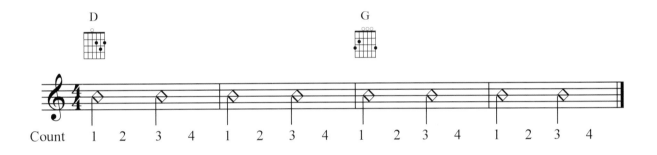

In this 3/4 time exercise, the half note is played on the first beat of the measure and is valued at two beats.

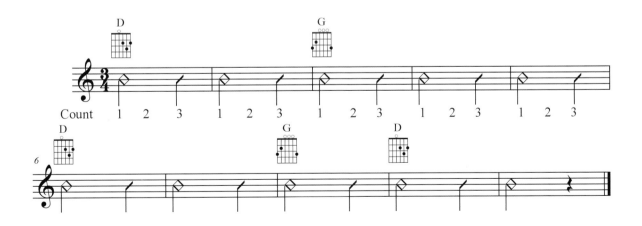

6. Basic Warm-up

Let's try to put together some of what you've just learned. Using chords we've learned already, let's try playing a short song. Remember the difference between the up stroke and down stroke symbol. Practice slowly until you feel like you're getting the hang of this exercise. When you're feeling comfortable with chord changes, you're ready to try playing a few songs that you're probably familiar with.

Exercise: G and D chord changes

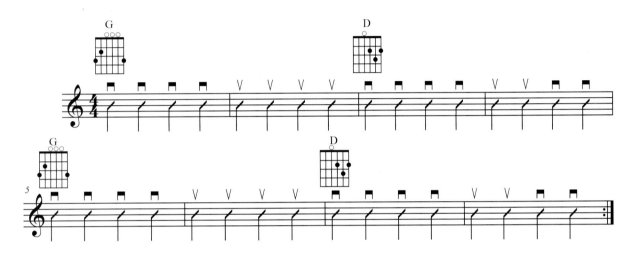

HELPFUL TIP for switching chords: As you go from G to D, your 3 finger moves ever so slightly to go to the second string, third fret. Slide your 1 and 2 fingers over to their positions.

7. G and D Exercises

Exercises: G to G7 switch

Let's try playing first in 4/4 time.

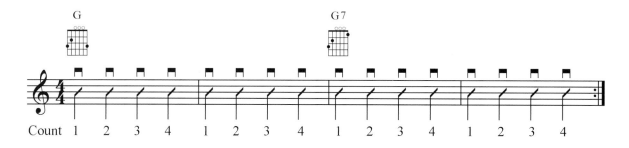

Here you have three beats to the measure.

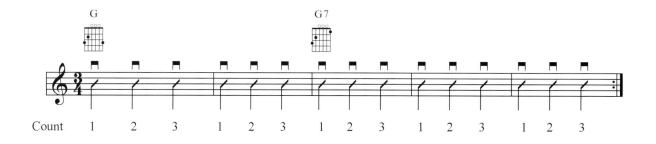

HELPFUL TIP:
When switching from G to G7, both your 1 and 3 fingers move from one side of the fret board to the other.

Song of the D's

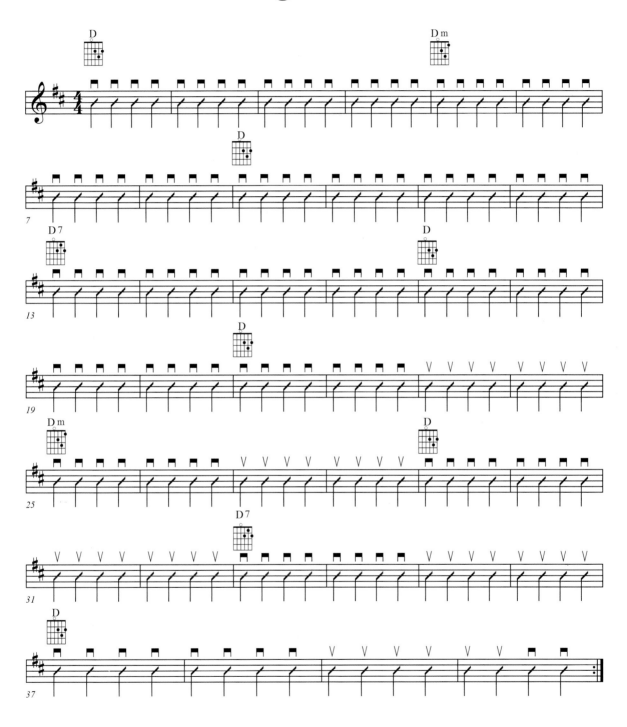

8. Reading Guitar Pieces in Tablature

Tablature is another way to read music for the guitar. When you see music written in tablature you will see TAB at the start of the music and not a bass or treble clef. This tells you right away that the song will be in tablature. A song can and will be written in both, as you will see.

In reading tablature you will see there are six horizontal lines. The lines represent the six strings of the guitar. The top line is the high E string, the second from the top is the B string, and so on. On the lines will be numbers. The number on the line indicates what fret to play on that string. If the first string has a number 1 on it, it means to press you finger on the first string at just about the middle of the first fret.

The numbers on the staff tell you what fret to place your fingers on. (A zero (0) on the string means to play the string open.) The numbers below the staff tell you what finger to use to play the note.

On the opposite page are three well-known songs written in tablature that you can use to practice. Nearly all of the other songs in this book will be written both ways, showing chord diagrams and musical notation as well as TAB form. This allows you to practice and play both styles. It also allows you to play with another guitarist.

Amazing Grace

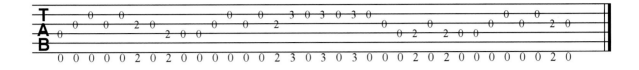

Jingle Bells

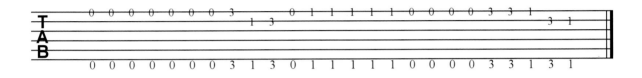

Row, Row, Row Your Boat

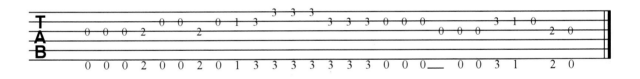

HELPFUL TIP:
If you want to jam with another guitar player, one of you can play the melody (reading the TAB staff) while the other strums the chords above the musical staff.

Remember, the dotted half note gets three beats. In 3/4 time, that means a dotted half note plays for the full measure.

Clementine

Stephen Foster

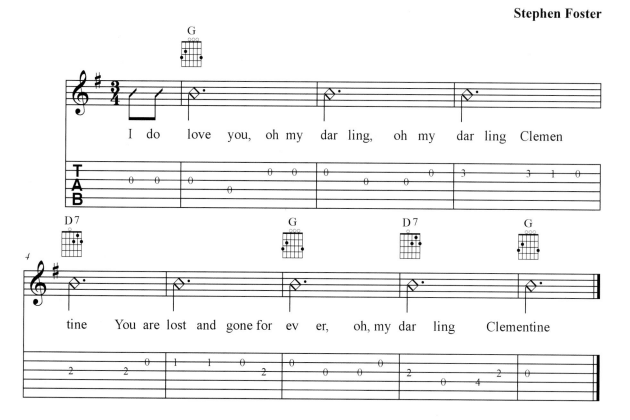

HELPFUL TIP:
When you see a dot in front of a note, such as in the 2nd, 5th, 6th, 8th, 9th, and 11th measures of this song, that means you should add one-half the original value of the note. So the dotted half notes in this song are played for three beats.

Did You Ever See a Lassie

Germany

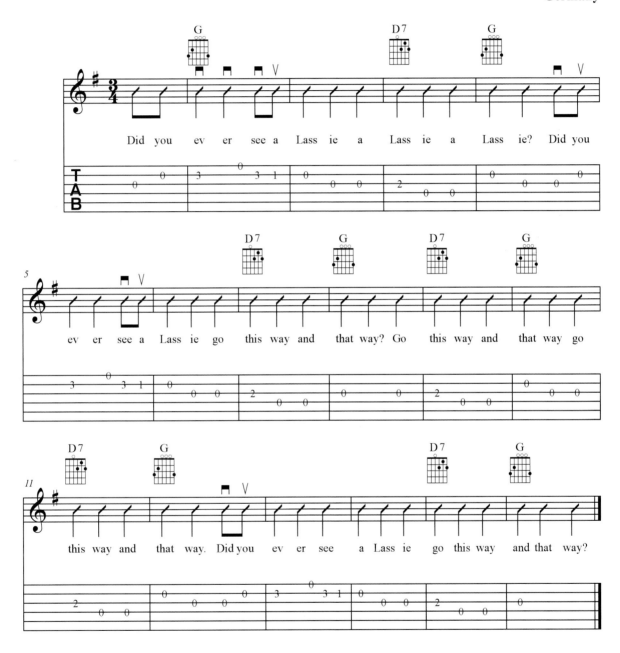

Down in the Valley

American Folk

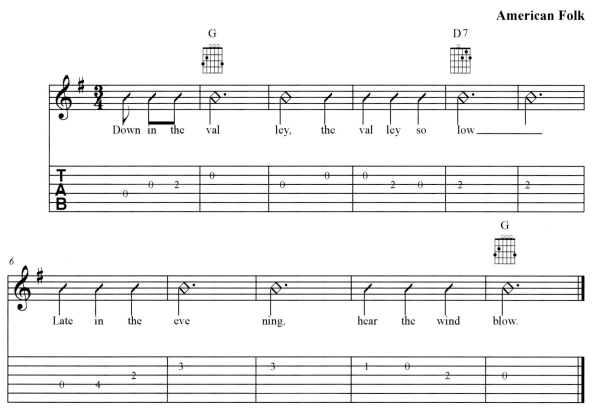

Down in the val ley, the val ley so low _____

Late in the eve ning, hear the wind blow.

YOU SHOULD KNOW:
The songs for this book were chosen for their worldwide appeal. While some tunes are unmistakably American, other songs come from the British Isles, Europe, Africa, the Caribbean, and even Japan.

9. Two New Chords: C and F

The next two chords, C and F, are among the most common you will learn. The C chord is pretty simple, but the F chord will take practice.

The C7 chord

    1 finger, second string, first fret
    2 finger, fourth string, second fret
    3 finger, fifth string, third fret

The C7 chord

The C7 chord is easy to play once you've mastered the C chord. To play a C7 chord, the fingering is the same as the C chord, just place your pinky on the third string, third fret.

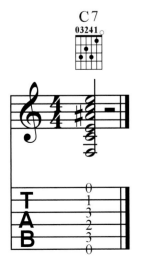

The F chord can be played two ways. One way is to bar the chord (that is, use one finger to press all the strings on a fret).

Before practicing this chord, try to simply bar all six strings along one fret. After you have mastered this, the rest of the chord goes like this:

2 finger, third string, second fret
3 finger, fourth string, third fret
4 finger, fifth string, third fret

The second way to play the F chord is shown below:

1 finger, first and second strings, first fret
2 finger, third string, second fret
3 finger, fourth string, third fret

Practice switching from the C chord to the F chord

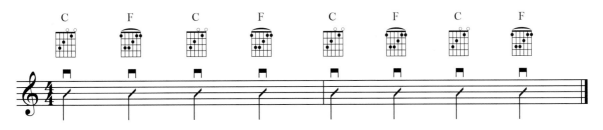

Try this exercise slowly at first. As you feel comfortable, increase the tempo.

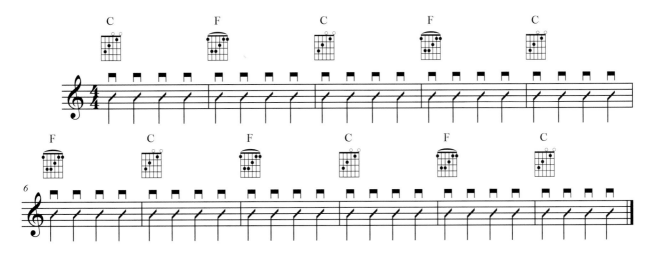

Watch as you play each chord every two beats:

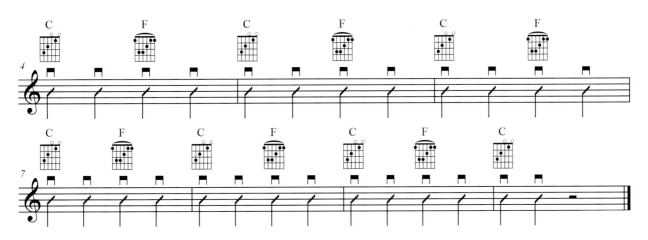

Exercise: changing between the C and C7 chords

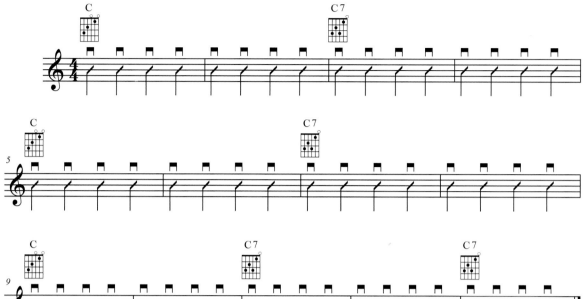

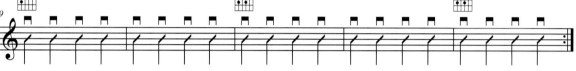

Exercise: C, G, and G7 chord changes

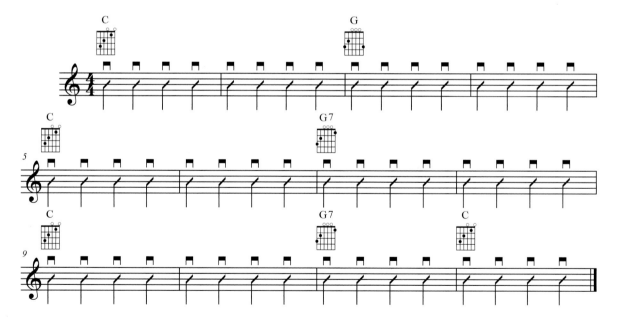

Exercise: playing with G, D, and C

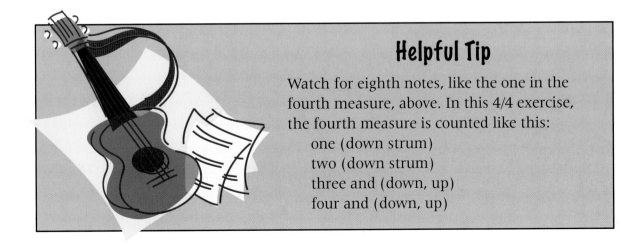

Helpful Tip

Watch for eighth notes, like the one in the fourth measure, above. In this 4/4 exercise, the fourth measure is counted like this:

one (down strum)

two (down strum)

three and (down, up)

four and (down, up)

Now you're ready to play some more complex exercises and songs. The music on the next few pages uses all of the chords that you've learned so far.

Mother, Mother

Here we use the chords C, F, D, and G

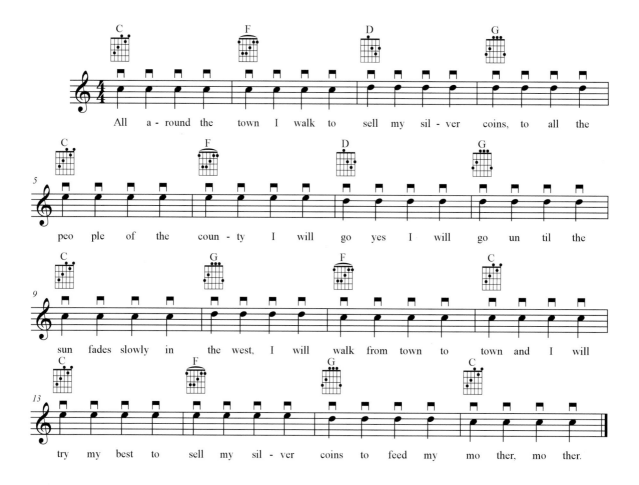

All a-round the town I walk to sell my sil-ver coins, to all the

peo-ple of the coun-ty I will go yes I will go un-til the

sun fades slowly in the west, I will walk from town to town and I will

try my best to sell my sil-ver coins to feed my mo-ther, mo-ther.

Camptown Races

Stephen Foster

Old MacDonald Had a Farm

American

Banyan Tree

Here is a simple song in 3/4 time

Jamaica

Did You Know?

While tinkering with designs for a solid body electric guitar, Les Paul fitted a railroad tie with steel strings and a pickup. In describing the guitar's sustain, he said, "You could go out to eat and come back and the note would still be sounding."

Tipalo Bend

American folk

Jacob's Ladder

Spiritual

10. New Chords: E, Em, and E7

Next, let's take a look at some more chords. Here you have the E, Em, and E7 chords. They are easy to play and each just as important as the others. As you play them, listen to the slightly different sound they make by just moving one finger.

The E Chord
    1 finger, first fret, third string
    2 finger, second fret, fifth string
    3 finger, second fret, fourth string

The Em Chord
    (Lift your 1 finger)
    2 finger, second fret, fifth string
    3 finger, second fret, fourth string

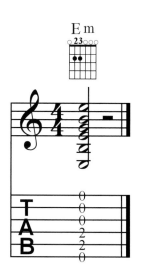

The E7 Chord

(Place first finger back where it was first fret, third string, and lift your third finger)

   1 finger, first fret, third string

   2 finger, second fret, fifth string

Use the exercises on the next page to practice changing between these three variations on the E chord.

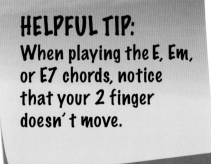

HELPFUL TIP:
When playing the E, Em, or E7 chords, notice that your 2 finger doesn't move.

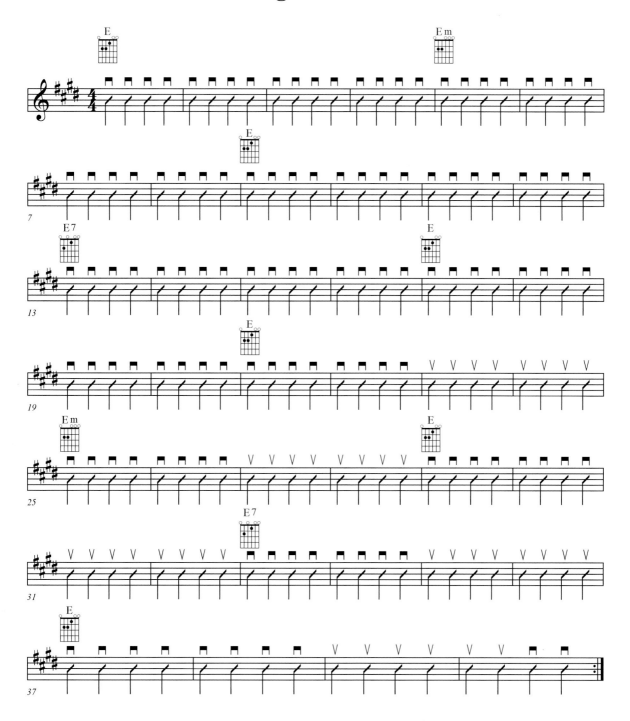

Song of the E's

Watch the 3/4 time

Major Chording In 3/4

Did You Know?

Legendary bluesman B.B. King named his Gibson hollow body guitar Lucille after having to save it from a fire that started in a club because of two men fighting over a woman of the same name.

Good King Wenceslas

Traditional European

11. The Family of A

The As:

Here you have the A, Am, and A7 chords. They are easy to play and again, just as important. They also sound slightly different when you move just one finger.

The A Chord

    2 finger, second fret, fourth string

    3 finger, second fret, third string

    4 finger, second fret, second string

HELPFUL TIP:

Place your 2 finger on the lower middle part of the second fret, fourth string. Your 3 finger goes in the middle of the second fret, third string. Your 4 finger presses the upper middle part of the second fret, second string.

Am

(Lift the 4 finger and place the 1 finger on the first fret, second string)
1 finger, first fret, second string
2 finger, second fret, fourth string
3 finger, second fret, third string

A7

(2 finger stays)
2 finger, second fret, fourth string
3 finger, second fret, second string

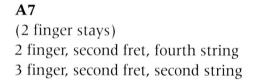

Use the exercise on the following pages to practice changing between the major, minor, and seventh chords:

Exercise: A, Am, and A7 chord changes

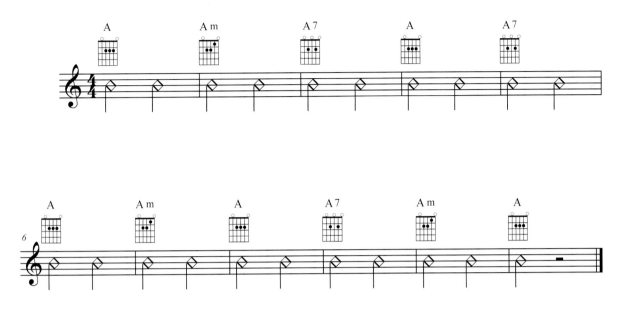

Tips for Switching Between the A, Am, and A7 Chords

When going from Am to A7, lift your 1 finger, move your 3 finger to the second string, second fret, and don't move your 2 finger.

When going from A to Am, lift the 4 finger up and put your 1 finger down on the second string, first fret. Your 2 and 3 fingers don't move.

When going from A7 to A, move your 3 finger to the third string, second fret, and place your 4 finger on the second string, second fret. Your 2 finger doesn't move

When going from Am to A, lift your 1 finger and place your 4 finger on the second string, second fret. Your 2 finger doesn't move.

When going from A7 to Am, lift your 3 finger and place it on the third string, second fret. Place your 1 finger on the second string, first fret. The 2 finger doesn't move.

Exercise: practicing 7th chords

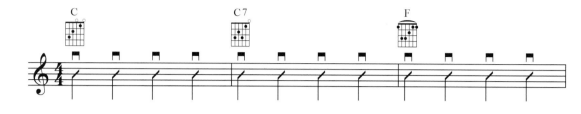

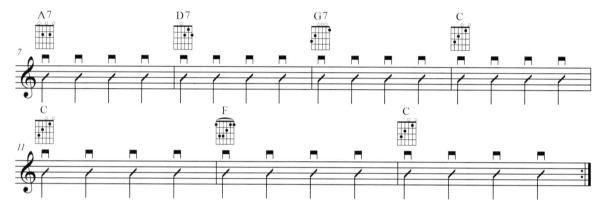

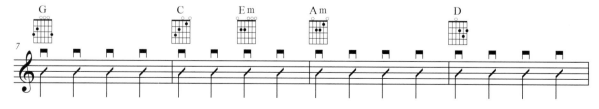

Exercise: practicing minor chords

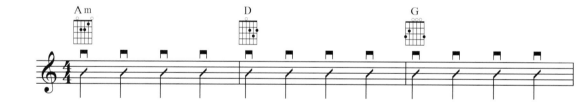

Song of the A's

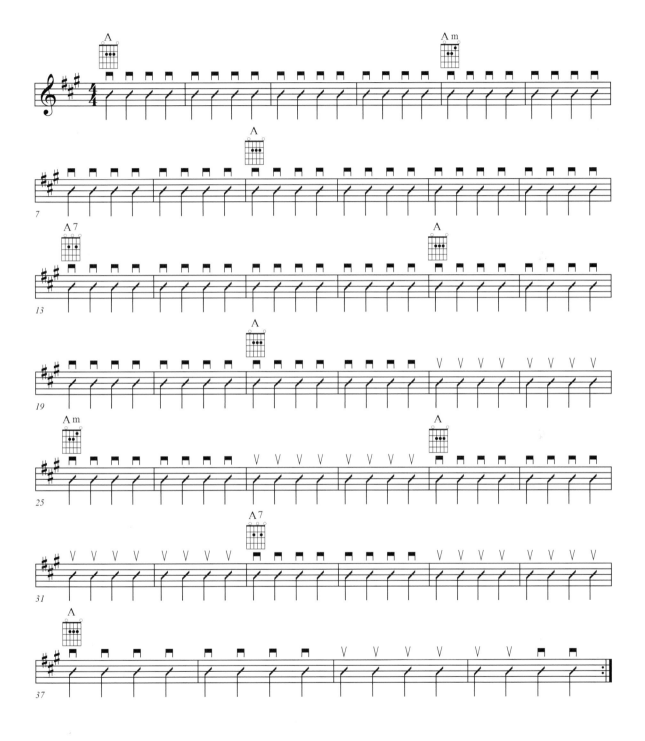

These are English lyrics
set to the French tune "Alouette."
You use the chords A and E7

All the Children

French melody

A   E 7   A   E 7   A

All the children, all the little children,   all the children,   children of the world. I can

E 7   A   E 7   E 7

see the sun today, I can see the sun today,   sun   to   day,   all the day,   So,

A   E 7   A   E 7   A

Little   children,   all the little children,   little children,   children of the world.

Did You Know?

Because very few left-handed guitars were available, Jimi Hendrix was forced to string his right-handed guitars upside down in order to play them.

This song is in the Key of D
Watch going from A to A7

Golden Slumbers

Traditional English

Gol — den slum — bers kiss — your eyes. ___ Smi les a

wait ___ you when ___ you rise. ___ Sleep pret ty wan ___ tons,

do ___ not cry ___ and I will ___ sing ___ a lu ___ la by ___

Watch the quick change of chords
at the end of the second measure.
The D7 is played on the fourth beat.
This also happens at the end of the
fourteenth measure

This Train

American Negro Spiritual

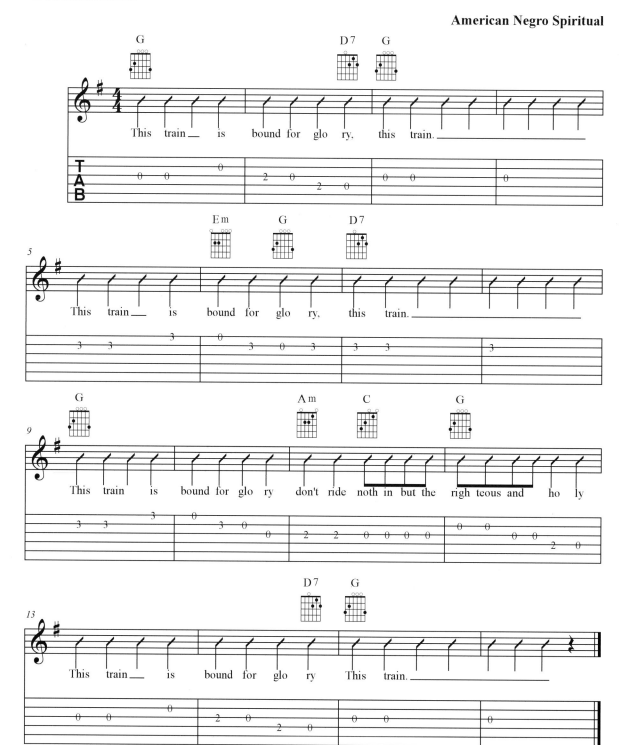

Blow the Man Down

American

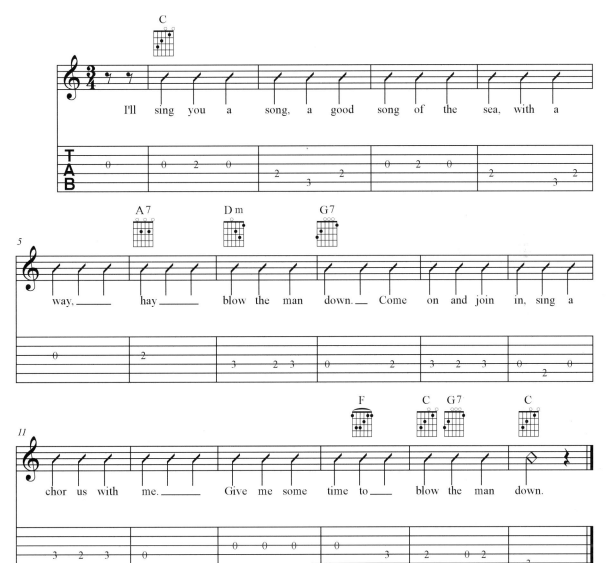

Did You Know?

Guitar picks have been made from any of a variety of materials, including nylon, rubber, plastic, felt, tortoise shell, metal, wood, and stone.

12. One More Chord (B7)

Now all we have to do is learn one more chord and you will know the chords to hundreds of songs.

The B7 Chord
1 finger, first fret, fourth string
2 finger, second fret, fifth string
3 finger, second fret, third string
4 finger, second fret, first string

The Blues

Next we have what is called a **12 bar blues** tune. This 12 bar blues pattern is the template for many great songs, from "Johnny B. Goode" to "Kansas City" to "Shake, Rattle, and Roll." Use the notation and add the rhythm.

The most important thing here is to make sure you are keeping in rhythm and following the beat. Take it slow and you will gradually pick it up.

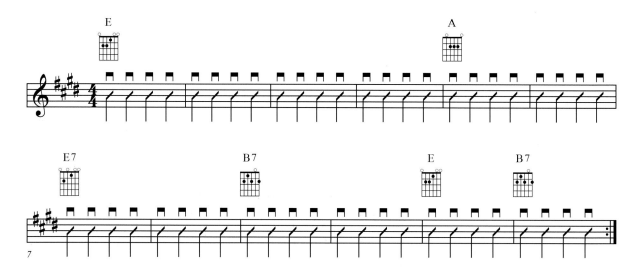

13. Playing with the Chords You Know

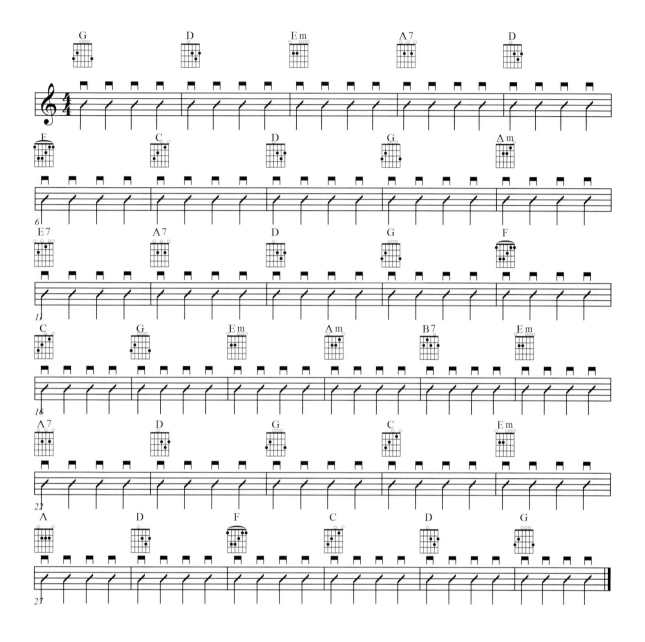

Exercise: Am, D, D7, G, G7, E, E7, A

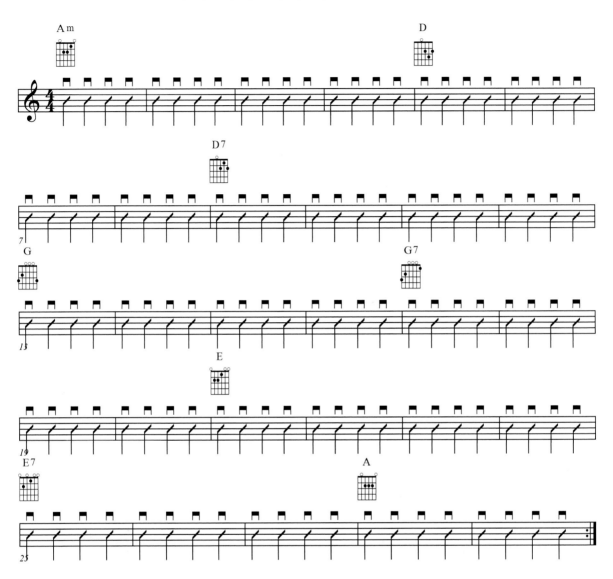

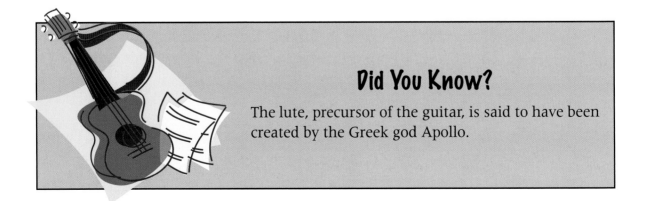

Did You Know?

The lute, precursor of the guitar, is said to have been created by the Greek god Apollo.

Exercise: Dm, A7, E7, G, D. Watch the 3/4 time

Pat-a-Pan

French carol

Wil lie take your lit - tle drum, Rob - in, bring your fife and come. Play - ing on the fife and drum, tu - re - lu - re - lu. - Pat - a - pat a pan, we'll make mu - sic loud and gay, for our Christ - mas hol - i - day.

Loch Lomond, Ye Take the High Road

Scotland

In the second, fifth, sixth, and twelfth measures, play the second eighth note with an upstroke, and all other notes as down strokes.

Here you play the
quarter strum 4 times
in each measure.
Keep the tempo even.

It's About the Time

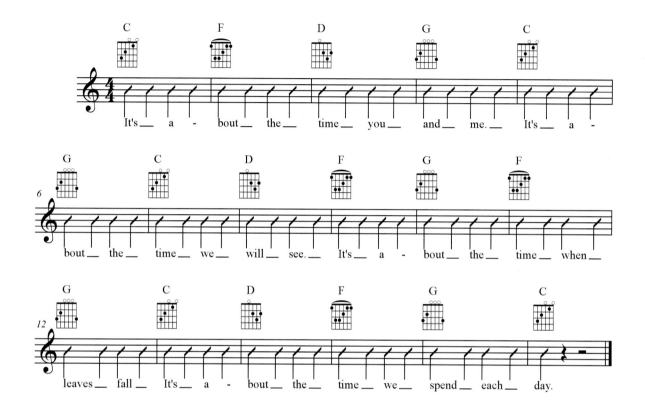

It's__ a - bout__ the__ time__ you__ and__ me.__ It's__ a -

bout__ the__ time__ we__ will__ see.__ It's__ a - bout__ the__ time__ when__

leaves__ fall__ It's__ a - bout__ the__ time__ we__ spend__ each__ day.

Did You Know?

The Yardbirds' manager, Giorgio Gomelsky, gave Eric Clapton the nickname "Slowhand." Clapton often broke strings during performances, and audiences would make fun of him by doing a slow hand-clap while he changed them onstage.

She'll Be Coming 'Round the Mountain

American

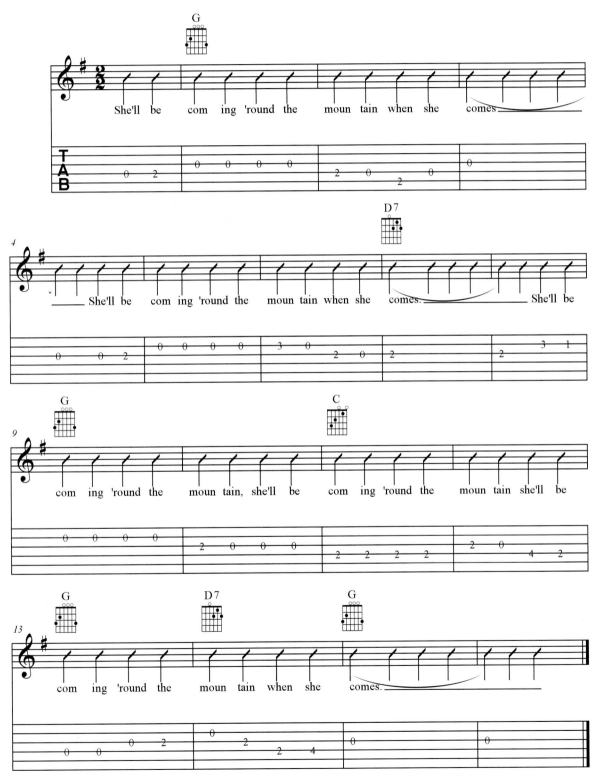

Accent the first, second, and
third beats at measures 9 and 10

Little Brown Jug

Traditional

Watch and prepare for
the third, seventh,
and fifteenth measures

Au Clair de la Lune

French

PART THREE:

BEYOND CHORDS

1. Exploring the Rest of the Basics

We've only barely begun to dive into the world of music. As we press on, you will see that what you are learning will allow you to communicate with musicians all around the world.

You have already seen the staff. Now we're going to learn what the placement of each note tells us. It's quite simple really, as music uses the letters A through G in a cycle. We'll start with the notes on the lines. The bottom line is the note E, the next line up is G, the next line up is B, the next is D, and the top line is F. To remember this order many young students memorize a phrase like "**E**very **G**ood **B**oy **D**eserves **F**udge."

The spaces from the bottom up are F, A, C, E. This is easy to remember, as it spells out the word "face."

If you can't remember one or two notes, don't worry; just remember that music uses only seven letters, A through G. If you can find a starting place on the staff, you can figure out which note you are looking at.

You can find notes *on* the staff, *above* the staff, and *below* the staff, as shown at the top of the opposite page.

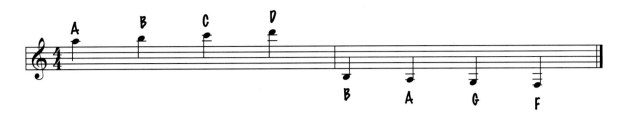

In the example above, some of the notes have an extra line or two through them, either above or below the five-line staff. These are called ledger lines, and they help the musician to easily identify the proper note.

One other thing you may see when you are reading music is a small number at the beginning of some measures (circled in red below). This is just a helpful guide for the musician; it lets you know what measure you are playing. This can be particularly useful when you are playing music with a group and the leader or instructor wants you to start at a particular measure, rather than at the beginning of the song. Although in this book the number appears above the staff at the first measure of each line of music, in other music you may find that the number appears at the bottom of the staff, or that each measure is numbered.

2. The Notes

Next we shall take a closer look at the notes that appear on the staff. The notes tell us what tones to play, and take on the names of the lines or spaces they occupy. A note has three parts.

The Head: gives a general indication of time: a hollow oval indicates a half note or a whole note, while a solid oval denotes a quarter, eighth, or other note.

The Stem: all notes except for whole notes have a stem.

The Flag: the presence of a flag indicates an eighth or sixteenth note.

A quarter note has a stem and a solid oval head. It usually gets one count. If there are four beats in the measure, you might count "one, two, three, four" in your mind when playing; the quarter note would generally be played for the amount of time it takes to count "one."

Quarter Note

Half Note

Eighth Note

Whole Note

Notes with a stem and hollow oval head are called half notes. A half note gets two counts, or beats, per measure. It is twice as long as a quarter note, so count "one, two."

An eighth note has a solid head, a stem, and a flag. Often, two eighth notes will be connected. The eighth note lasts half as long as a quarter note. So if you are mentally counting the beats in the measure, you would count "one and two and three and four and." Each of these words would represent an eighth note; you would play on the "one" but not on the "and," for example.

A whole note is a hollow circle. It indicates a note that receives four beats.

Sometimes, you will see a dot next to a note, as shown in the lower left corner. This means that when you play the note, you need to add one-half the original value of the note to its length. For example, a dotted half note is played for three beats, while a dotted quarter note is extended by an extra eighth. (In 4/4 time each measure would have eight eighth notes; the dotted quarter note would be played for three eighths.)

Rests also appear in the measure. These symbols indicate to the musician when he or she should take a brief break from playing. Like notes, there are different symbols for rests, depending on how long the musician should be silent. Two common rests, quarter note and half note rests, are pictured below. A whole note rest looks like a half note rest, except that it drops below the third line on the staff, rather than rising above it.

Dotted Half Note

Quarter Note Rest

Half Note Rest

3. Clef Symbols

In the previous section, specific notes were assigned to the lines and spaces on the staff. The way that you can be sure what note each line or space represents is to look at the beginning of the first staff of music. There, you will see a symbol called a clef. There are several different clef symbols; each indicates to the person reading the music which notes the lines and spaces on the staff represent. For the guitar you will only need to know one, the treble, or G, clef. When you see the treble clef, you'll know that the notes on the lines are EGBDF and the notes on the spaces are FACE.

Another commonly used clef is the bass clef, but this is mostly found in piano and bass instrument music. While we won't be covering how to read bass clef in this book, it's still good to know the symbol in case you ever come across it. The lines and spaces in bass clef have different note values than the lines and spaces in treble clef.

The Treble Clef

The Bass Clef

4. Time Signature

In addition to the clef, there is also a time signature written at the beginning of the musical staff. The time signature tells the musician how many beats are in each measure and which note is valued at one beat.

The top number indicates the number of beats per measure. So in 4/4 time, there are four beats per measure, while in 3/4 time there are three beats per measure. The bottom number tells which note gets one beat. A 4 on the bottom of the time signature means the quarter note gets one beat. In 6/8 time each measure would have 6 beats and the eighth note would be played as one beat.

Below are some examples of time signatures that are often used in guitar music. You will sometimes see a C in the place of a time signature. That simply stands for 4/4, or common time. Most of the music you will see will be written either in 4/4 or 3/4 time.

2/4 Time

4/4 Time
(also known as common time)

3/4 Time

6/8 Time

Let's Review

1. Music is written on a **staff**, which has **five** lines and **four** spaces.
2. The notes of the lines are **EGBDF.**
3. The notes of the spaces are **FACE.**
4. Guitar music is normally written in the **treble clef.**
5. The staff is divided into **measures** by vertical lines called **bars**.

5. More Chords

Below are the chords we have already looked at, but this time they are written out using musical notation.

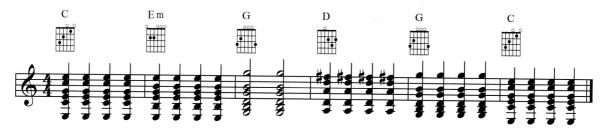

You have the bar line, then the clef, then the time signature, then the key signature. The key of C has no sharps or flats, so the key signature is empty in the example above.

6. The Sharp and Flat Signs

The figure on the F line on the staff to the right is called a sharp. If you see it placed in front of a note, you should play the note a half step up. For example, if you see an F with the # before it, you would not play F, you would play the note a half tone higher. This note is called F#.

 Notes can also be flat, which means they are played a half tone lower. A flat sign looks like a small b (pictured at left). As you've probably figured out, sharps and flats can indicate the same tone. The note G is one step above F, so you use the same fingering to play F# (a half-step up) and Gb (a half-step down). These are known as enharmonic notes.

The first place you will see flats and sharps is in the key signature. If you see one sharp in the key signature (like in the first image in this section) the music is in the key of G. If you see one flat in the key signature (as in the second image in this section), the music is in the key of F. Below are the sharps and flats that will appear in the key signatures of some other musical keys.

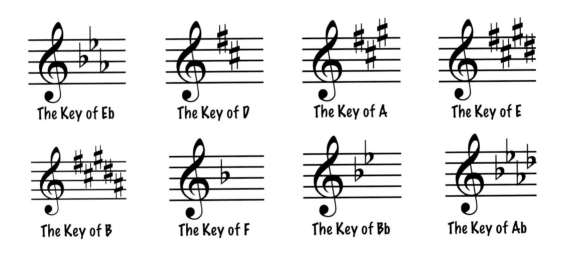

The Key of Eb   The Key of D   The Key of A   The Key of E

The Key of B   The Key of F   The Key of Bb   The Key of Ab

Sometimes a song may include a note or notes that are not in the same key as the rest of the song. When this happens, you will see a sharp or flat symbol next to the note in your music. If the note is already sharp or flat, you may see another symbol next to the note. This means to play the natural tone. Musicians call these notes "accidentals."

Natural Symbol

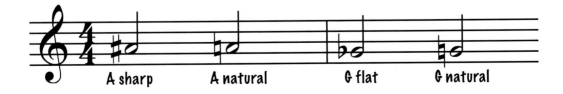

A sharp   A natural   G flat   G natural

7. String Notation

We already know what strings are on the guitar: remember EADGBE. Now we'll review the basic notes that can be played from these strings.

The E String

From the earlier chapters you know that both the first and sixth strings on the guitar play the note E. We'll start with what guitar players call the first string and is the thinnest of the strings.

8. The E (First String) and its Notes

The first note E is played on the open string.

The second note is F. It is played by pressing the first fret with the 1 finger, as in the picture below:

The third note on the high E string is G, played by pressing the third fret with the 3 finger, as pictured:

Following are three practice exercises:

The Easy E

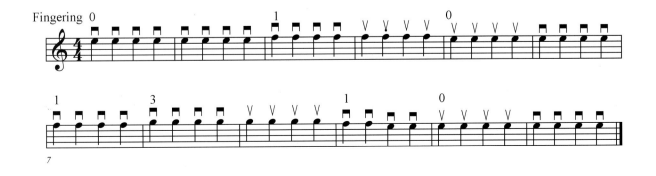

The E's a Changing

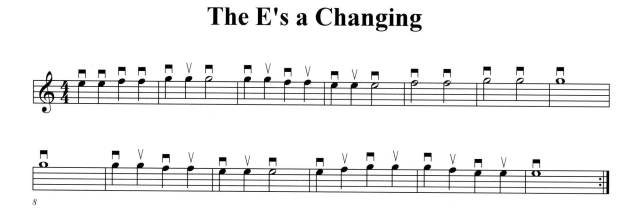

The E's to Go

Did You Know?

A typical mariachi band will include at least three kinds of guitar—a classical guitar, a vihuela (a five-string guitar) and a guitarron, a large guitar that is nearly the size of a cello.

9. The B String and its Notes

The first note B is played by playing the open string.

The second note is C played by pressing the first fret with the 1 finger. (See image below.)

The third note on the B string is D, which is played by pressing the third fret with the 3 finger.

The Baby B string

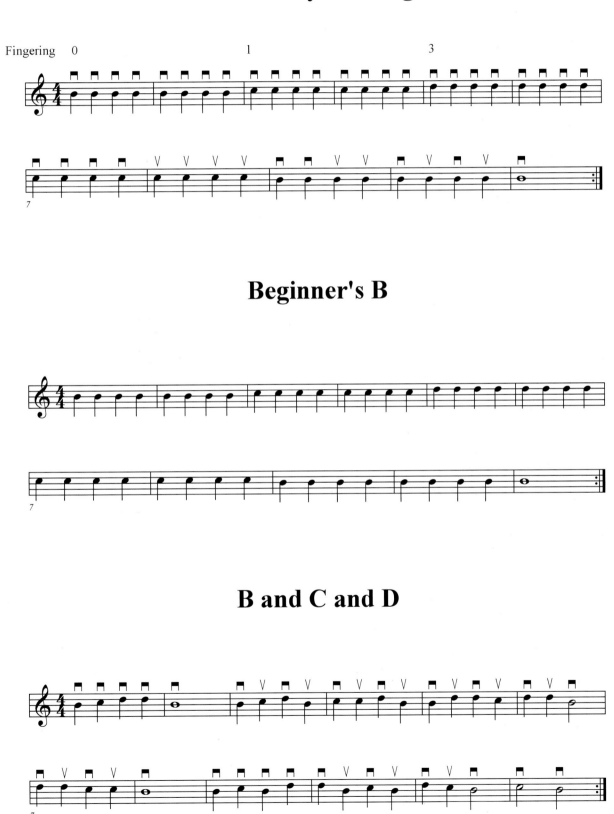

Beginner's B

B and C and D

10. The G String and its Notes

The first note, G, is played by playing the open string.

The second note is A, played by pressing the second fret with the 2 finger. (See image below.)

Gee It's Nice

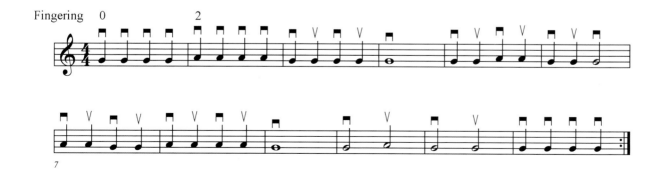

7

G and A

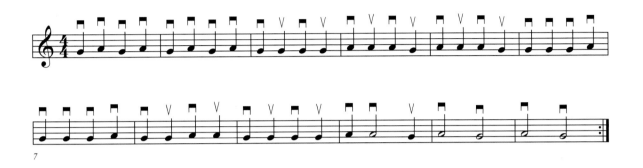

This next song uses the top three strings. Take your time and try not to look at your fingers.

The Upper String March

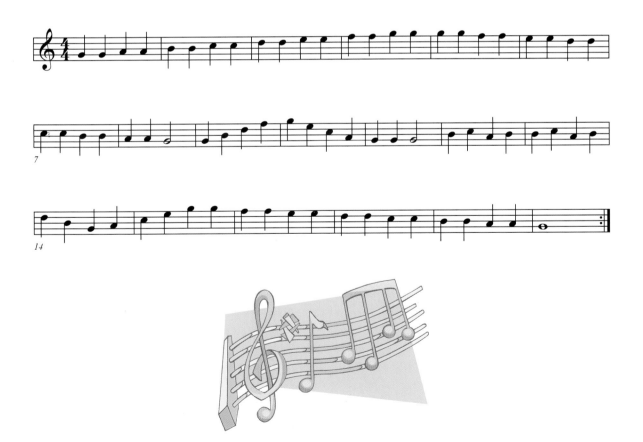

11. The D String and its Notes

The first note, D, is played by playing the open string.

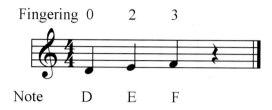

The second note is E, played by pressing the second fret with the 2 finger. (As shown below.)

The third note is F, played by pressing the third fret with the 3 finger. (As shown below.)

Did You Know?

Django Reinhardt was forced to create a new fingering system after an injury sustained in a fire caused him to lose the use of the fourth and fifth fingers on his left hand.

Easy D

Daring Three

Doing It Well

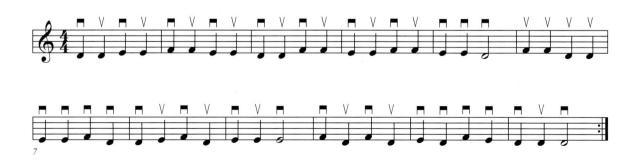

12. The A String and its Notes

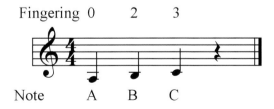

The first note, A, is played by playing the open string.

The second note, B, is played by pressing the second fret with the 2 finger. (See image above.)

The third note is C, and it is played by pressing the third fret with the 3 finger. (As shown on the opposite page, top.)

An Easy Ride

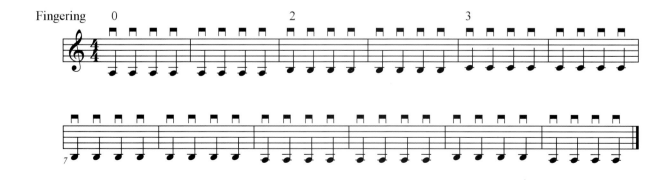

A Lesson Well

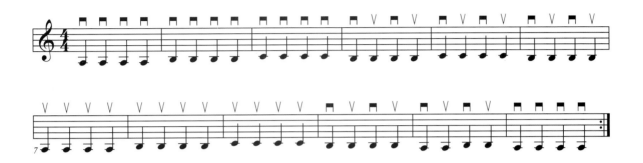

A through C

13. The E String and its Notes

The first note, E, is played by playing the open string.

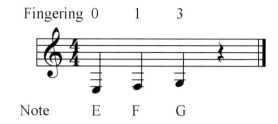

The second note is F, played by pressing the first fret with the 1 finger. (See below left for an example of the proper fingering.)

The third note is G, played by pressing the third fret with the 3 finger. (As in the example on the lower right.)

Easy Low

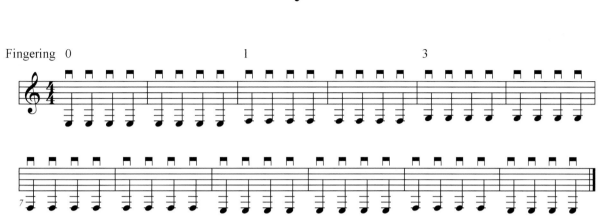

Early Bird

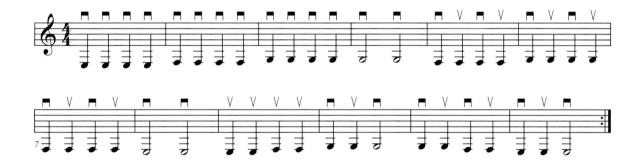

Easy Bass

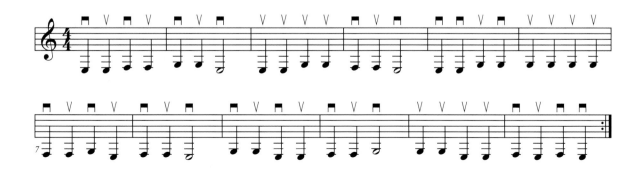

Notes of the Low Strings

Half Notes on the Low strings

The Low String Walk

Really Getting Low

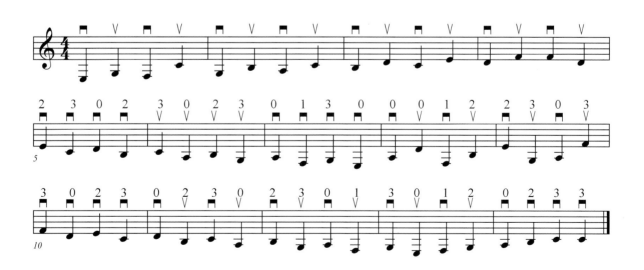

PART FOUR

MORE SONGS

The following section contains a number of well-known songs which you can practice—and maybe even play for your friends or family some day. In addition to the chord diagrams, the melodies are written in standard notation as well as tablature, to help you if you want to practice picking out the tunes.

Remember, all great guitarists started as beginners. Enjoy making music!

Kumbaya

Africa

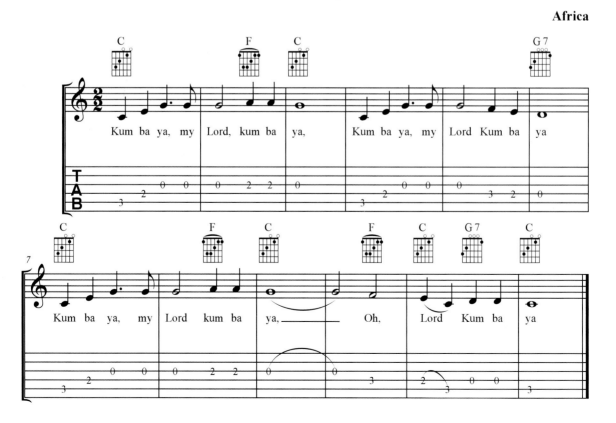

My Bonnie

England

Cielito Lindo

Mexico

From si er___ra Mo re na, cie___ li to Lin do, comes

___soft ly steal___ Laugh ing eyes so black and ro guish. Cie___

___li to Lin do, beau___ty re veal ing.___ Ay, ay, ay,

ay,___ sing me your sor row___ To pass the hours

___soft ly sing ing. Cie___ li to night we sing___ of the mor row___

Bingo

Scotland

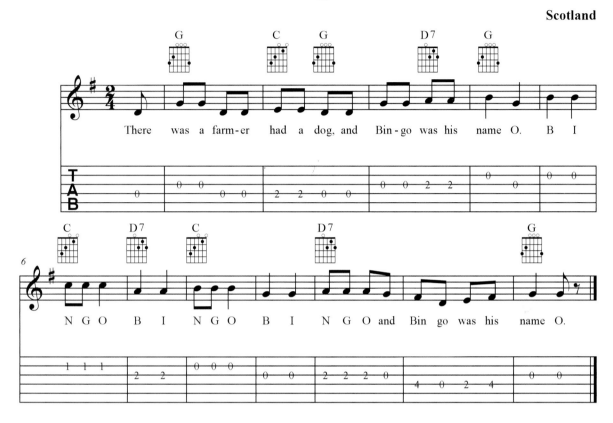

On Top of Old Smokey

American folk song

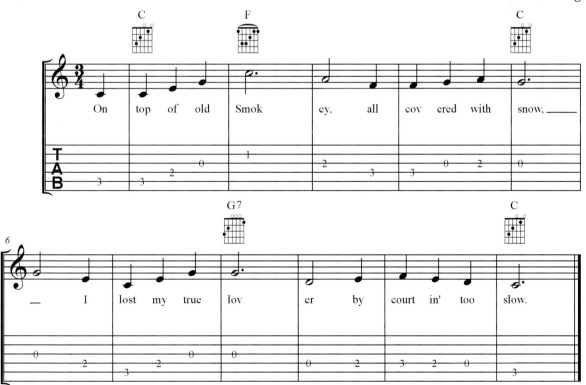

At the Gate of Heaven

Spain

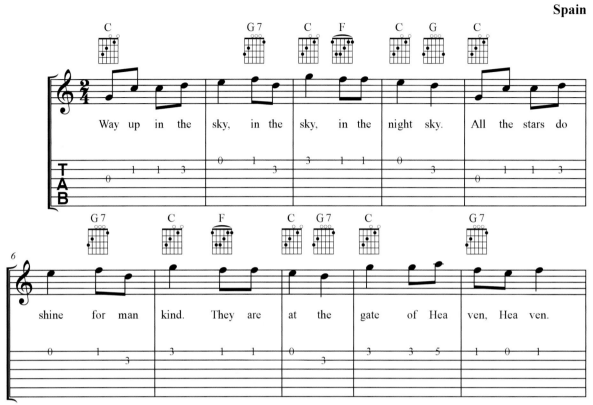

This Old Man

Traditional English

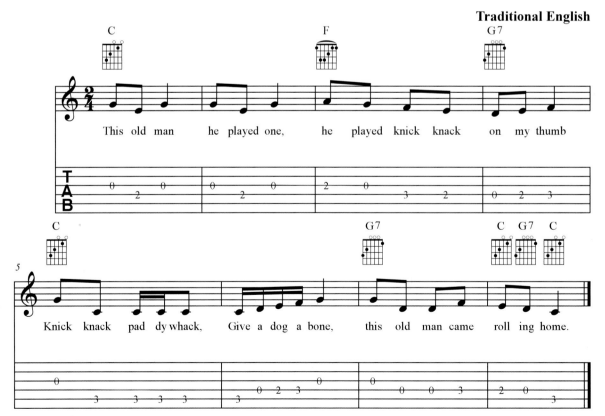

Red River Valley

Cowboy

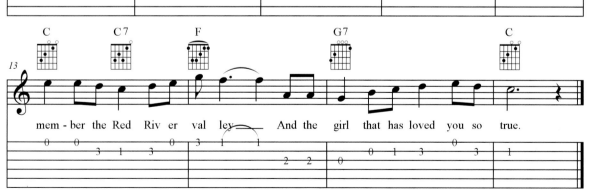

APPENDIX: CHORD DIAGRAMS

A
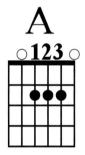

A m
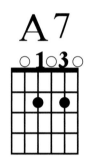

A 7
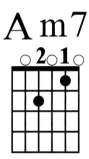

A m7
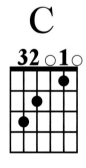

B♭
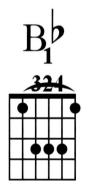

B 7

B m
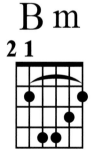

C

C 7

D

D m

D 7

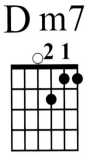

D m7

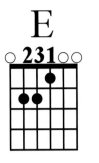

E

E m

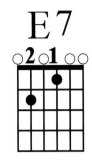

E 7

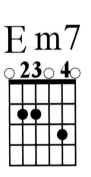

E m7

F

G

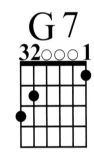

G 7

GUITAR TIMELINE

1400 B.C.: Evidence suggests that a four string, guitar-like instrument was played by the Hittites (who occupied the region now known as Asia Minor and Syria). According to this theory, the Spanish guitar derived from the *tanbur* of the Hittites, *kithara* of the Greeks, and later the *cithara* of the Romans.

A.D. 1200: The four string guitar had evolved into two types: the *guitarra morisca* (Moorish guitar) which had a rounded back, wide fingerboard, and several sound holes, and the *guitarra latina* (Latin guitar), which resembled the modern guitar with one sound hole and a narrower neck.

1265: Juan Gil of Zamora mentions the early guitar in *Ars Musica*.

1306: A "gitarer" was played at the Feast of Westminster in England.

ca. 1350: Guitarra latina and guitarra morisca are mentioned multiple times in the poems of the Archpriest of Hita.

1404: *Der mynnen regein* by Eberhard Von Cersne makes reference to a "quinterne."

1400s: The vihuela was born late in this century by adding doubled strings and increasing its size. It was a large plucked instrument with a long neck (vibrating string length: 72 to 79 cm) with ten or eleven frets and six pairs of strings.

1546: *Tres Libros de Musica en Cifras para Vihuela* by Alonso Mudarra is the first publication to include music for guitar.

1551–55: Adrian Le Roy publishes nine books of tablature. These include the first pieces for five-course guitar. The addition of the fifth course was attributed to Vicente Espinel.

1600–50: Many publications of tablature for the guitar start to appear. Its popularity begins to rival the lute.

1674: Publication of *Guitarre Royal* by F. Corbetta increased the guitar's popularity. It was dedicated to Louis XIV, who was an avid player of the guitar.

ca. 1770: A sixth string was added to the guitar and the double strings were replaced by single strings.

1800–50: The guitar enjoyed great popularity both in performances and publishing. Fernando Sor, Mauro Guiliani, Matteo Carcassi, and Dioniso Aguado all performed, taught, wrote, and published their compositions.

1850–92: Guitar maker Antonio de Torres develops the larger, more resonant instrument we know today.

1894: Orville Gibson introduces guitars with curved backs instead of flat ones, allowing for better volume and timbre.

1916: Andres Segovia performs at Ateneo, the most important concert hall in Madrid. Before this it was thought that the guitar did not have the volume for this type of venue.

1931: Adolph Rickenbacker invents the electric guitar. Known as the Frying Pan, it was a lap-steel guitar with an electromagnetic pickup, created by Rickenbacker and George Beauchamp, in which a current passed through a coil of wire wrapped around a magnet. This created a field that amplified the strings' vibrations. By the time production ceased in 1939, several hundred thousand had been produced.

1933: Vivi-tone introduces the world's first electric solid-body guitar, which is so ahead of its time that barely anyone pays attention to it.

1936: Robert Johnson performs the first of just two recording sessions conducted during his lifetime. Considered by some to be the "Grandfather of Rock 'n Roll," Johnson's vocal phrasing, original songs, and guitar style influenced a range of musicians, including Led Zeppelin, Bob Dylan, the Rolling Stones, U2, the White Stripes, and Eric Clapton, who called Johnson "the most important blues musician who ever lived."

1946: Django Reinhardt comes to America to play Carnegie Hall with Duke Ellington. Many other guitarists have cited Reinhardt as a major influence, including Jeff Beck, blues legend B.B. King, the Grateful Dead's Jerry Garcia, Mark Knopfler, and Les Paul.

1950: Fender releases the Broadcaster and the Esquire, the first solid-body guitars designed with mass production in mind.

1952: Les Paul invents the Gibson guitar, the company's first solid-body electric guitar. Also, guitarist Jimmie Webster publishes a book entitled *The Touch System for Electric and Amplified Spanish Guitar*, outlining his unique two-handed tapping style.

1954: Fender releases the Stratocaster, which embodied a few new electric guitar design concepts, such as a radical new body design, a new pickup configuration, and an integral tailpiece/vibrato arm.

1955: Chuck Berry cuts his first rock and roll records. They are the first albums to feature the guitar as the main instrument. Berry also develops the descending pentatonic double-stops (the essence of rock guitar).

1957:   Link Wray's Rumble invents the "fuzz-tone" guitar sound.

1958:   Innovative guitarist Lowman Pauling incorporates guitar distortion and feedback into the Five Royales' single "The Slummer and the Slum." (The next group to use feedback and distortion in this manner was The Beatles, in their 1964 hit "I Feel Fine.")

1959:   Wes Montgomery does his first solo recordings. Along with the use of octaves (playing the same note on two strings) for which he is widely known, Montgomery was also an excellent single-line, or single-note player, and was very influential in the use of block chords in his solos.

1963:   Surf music, dominated by guitarist Dick Dale and the Deltones, rules the airwaves.

1964:   Bob Dylan plays an entirely electric set at the Newport Folk Music Festival, shocking his fans, most of whom either leave the venue or stay to boo him.

1967:   Jimi Hendrix performs at the Monterey Pop festival (his first major American performance) and burns his guitar during an encore performance of The Troggs' "Wild Thing." Hendrix is arguably the greatest and most influential electric guitarist in rock music history.

1978:   The rock group Van Halen releases its self-titled debut album. Guitarist Eddie Van Halen's two-handed tapping techniques, use of natural and artificial harmonics, speed, melodicism, and rhythmic sensibility influenced an entire generation of guitarists.

1981:   Stanley Jordan releases *Touch Sensitive*. Jordan's touch technique employs two-handed tapping. Both hands are positioned over the fretboard to tap notes on multiple strings. This method allows the guitarist to play melody and chords simultaneously.

1984:   Yngwie Johann Malmsteen, pioneer in the neo-classical metal genre, releases his seminal album *Rising Force*.

1987:   Freddie Green, who played with the Count Basie Orchestra, dies. Green was a peerless rhythm guitarist, whose reliable pulse propelled what many call the hardest swinging band in jazz.

2000:   Eric Clapton becomes the first person inducted into the Rock 'n Roll Hall of Fame three times. He was inducted as a member of the Yardbirds, a member of Cream, and as a solo artist.

2007:   Guitarist Tony Iommi announces that Rock 'n Roll Hall of Fame inductees Black Sabbath, forerunners of the heavy metal genre, will release new material and tour with their original lineup. The band, which began playing together almost 40 years ago, influenced such later groups as Alice in Chains, Soundgarden, Black Flag, Anthrax, Tenacious D, and Faith No More.

INTERNET RESOURCES

http://www.supersonic.net

> This website contains over 60 lessons, some of which are accompanied by audio files, covering a number of guitar and music related subjects ranging from guitar basics to music theory as well as forming your own band.

http://azchords.com

> Here you can find and request user-submitted tablature for thousands of songs, listed alphabetically by artist.

http://acapella.harmony-central.com/forums

> This highly informative online forum for musicians of all skill levels allows participants to share guitar playing tips, review musical equipment, discuss music industry-related issues, and read about dozens of other topics.

http://www.freeguitarvideos.com

> Professional guitarist Peter Vogl gives 85 free lessons with video accompaniment covering over 10 different styles of guitar playing. Techniques covered include blues, jazz, and country among many others.

http://www.musicgearreview.com

> Music Gear Review is an invaluable resource for musicians of all skill levels and experience, where users rate and review hundreds of pieces of musical equipment.

GLOSSARY

Bar lines—these vertical lines mark the division between measures of music.

Chord—three or more different tones played at the same time.

Clef (bass and treble)—located on the left side of each line of music, these symbols indicate the names and pitch of the notes corresponding to their lines and spaces.

Eighth note—a note with a solid oval, a stem, and a single tail that has 1/8 the value of a whole note.

Flat sign (b)—a symbol that indicates that the note following it should be lowered by one half step. This remains in effect for an entire measure, unless otherwise indicated by a natural sign.

Half note—a note with a hollow oval and stem that has 1/2 the value of a whole note.

Key signature—found between the clef and time signature, it describes which notes to play with sharps or flats throughout a piece of music.

Measure—a unit of music contained between two adjacent bar lines.

Notes—written or printed symbols which represent the frequency and duration of tones contained in a piece of music.

Pitch—the perceived highness or lowness of a sound or tone.

Quarter note—a note with a solid oval and a stem that is played for 1/4 of the duration of a whole note.

Sharp sign (#)—this symbol indicates that the note following it should be raised by one half-step. This remains in effect for an entire measure, unless otherwise indicated by a natural sign.

Time signature—located to the right of the clef and key signatures, the top digit indicates the number of beats per measure, and the number at the bottom shows which kind of note receives one beat.

Whole note—a note indicated by a hollow oval without a stem. It has the longest time value and represents a length of 4 beats when written in 4/4 time.

INDEX

"All the Children," 60
amplifier, 12
"At the Gate of Heaven," 102
"Au Clair de la Lune," 73

"Banyan Tree," 47
"Bingo," 101
"Blow the Man Down," 63

"Camptown Races," 45
chord diagram, 22, 23, 24, 25, 39, 40,
    50, 51, 55, 56, 64, 104–105
chords
    A (family) 55–59
    B7, 64
    C (family), 39, 41–43
    D (family), 24–25, 31–33
    E (family) 50–52
    F (family), 40–41
    G (family), 23–24, 31–32
"Cielito Lindo," 100
"Clementine," 36

"Did You Ever See a Lassie," 37
"Down in the Valley," 38

electronic tuning device, 18

folk music, 10
fret board, 10, 16, 19

"Golden Slumbers," 61
"Good King Wenceslas," 54
Guitar
    acoustic, 10, 11, 12, 20
    changing strings on, 20–21

electric, 10, 11, 12, 21
    holding and handling the, 15, 16
    strumming, 17, 28–29

hand techniques, 16

"It's About the Time," 70

"Jacob's Ladder," 49

"Kumbaya," 98

"Little Brown Jug," 72
"Loch Lomond, Ye Take the High Road,"
    69

"Mother, Mother," 44
"My Bonnie," 99

"Old MacDonald Had a Farm," 46
"On Top of Old Smokey," 101

"Pat-a-Pan," 68
pitch pipe, 18
practice, 9, 98

reading music, 26, 74–79
"Red River Valley," 103
rock music, 10

strings, 10
string notes
    A, 17, 26, 86, 91
    B, 17, 26, 83, 91
    C, 83, 91–92
    D, 17, 26, 83, 88
    E, 17, 26, 88, 94
    F, 80, 89, 94
    G, 17, 26, 81, 86, 94
    high E, 17, 26, 80
"She'll Be Coming 'Round the
    Mountain," 71
strumming, 17, 28–29

tablature, 22, 34–35, 98
"This Old Man," 102
"This Train," 62
time signature, 27
"Tipalo Bend," 48
12 bar blues, 64

ABOUT THE AUTHOR

Frank Cappelli is a warm, engaging artist, who possesses the special ability to transform the simple things of life into a wonderful musical experience. He has had an impressive career since receiving a B.A. in music education from West Chester State College (now West Chester University). Frank has performed his music at many American venues—from Disney World in Florida to Knott's Berry Farm in California—as well as in Ireland, Spain, France, and Italy. He has also performed with the Detroit Symphony, the Buffalo Philharmonic, the Pittsburgh Symphony, and the Chattanooga Symphony.

In 1987, Frank created Peanut Heaven, a record label for children. The following year, he worked with WTAE-TV in Pittsburgh to develop *Cappelli and Company*, an award winning children's television variety show. The weekly program premiered in 1989, and is now internationally syndicated.

In 1989, Frank signed a contract with A&M Records, which released his four albums for children (*Look Both Ways, You Wanna Be a Duck?, On Vacation,* and *Good*) later that year. *Pass the Coconut* was released by A&M in 1991. *Take a Seat* was released in September of 1993. With the 1990 A&M Video release of *All Aboard the Train and Other Favorites* and *Slap Me Five*, Cappelli's popular television program first became available to kids nationwide. Both videos have received high marks from a number of national publications, including *People Magazine, Video Insider, Billboard, USA Today, Entertainment Weekly,* and *TV Guide*.

Frank has received many awards, including the Parent's Choice Gold Award, regional Emmy Awards, the Gabriel Award for Outstanding Achievement in Children's Programming, and the Achievement in Children's Television Award. He is a three-time recipient of the Pennsylvania Association of Broadcasters' award for Best Children's Program in Pennsylvania.